You Cannot Yasin:

Written by
Cath Jones

Illustrated by
Leo Trinidad

Dash, dash dash!

Rush, rush, rush!

Yasin ran.

Dash, dash dash!

Rush, rush, rush!

Yasin ran!

Ring! Ring! Ring!

Dash, dash dash!

Rush, rush, rush!

Yasin ran!

He ran north, up the hill.

Then he ran back!

Dash, dash dash!

Rush, rush, rush!

Yasin ran into the fort at the top of the hill!

Dash, dash dash!

Rush, rush, rush!

Yasin ran with a torch.

Dash, dash dash!

Rush, rush, rush!

Yasin ran into a yurt.

Will Yasin get hurt in the yurt?

But then …

Yasin and Mum ran for the bus!